Pornography

Slaying the Dragon

D1372367

Resources for Changing Lives

A Ministry of
THE CHRISTIAN COUNSELING AND
EDUCATIONAL FOUNDATION
Glenside, Pennsylvania

RCL Ministry Booklets
Susan Lutz, Series Editor

Paul David Tripp, *Marriage: Whose Dream?*
David Powlison, *Pornography: Slaying the Dragon*
Edward T. Welch, *A.D.D.: Wandering Minds and Wired Bodies*

Pornography

Slaying the Dragon

An Interview
by

David Powlison

P&R
PUBLISHING
P.O. BOX 817 • PHILLIPSBURG • NEW JERSEY 08865-0817

© 1999 by David Powlison

Printed in the United States of America

ISBN 0-87552-677-2

Private sexual fantasy can dominate vast areas of a person's mental life. As explicit sexual images proliferate in films and magazines, on television, and over the Internet, the temptations increase and the bondage seems unbreakable. Even Christians can find that their lives have become a push-pull struggle between indulging in fantasy and resisting it.

Is it really possible to slay the dragon of pornography and fantasy once it has gained control of your life? In this interview by David Powlison, you will meet a man we will call Bob, who experienced Christ's deliverance in this part of his life.

DP: Bob, would you tell something of the history of your struggle with sexual fantasy?

BOB: From the age of thirteen or fourteen, I became fascinated with the female body. *Playboy* magazine was the only explicit material I had access to back in the 1960s. I began by developing fantasies about whoever was pictured in the magazine. Even though I knew it was wrong, I liked that experience. I liked the sense of power that came with enjoying the pictures. I found pornography intoxicating.

As the years went on and our culture became more promiscuous and permissive, the material I looked at became extremely explicit. I developed habits of masturbation, and I also developed elaborate sexual fantasies about women I actually knew. I'd look at pornography, and then overlay what I saw there onto female acquaintances. Eventually I constructed an entire "tape library" of imaginary fantasy tapes about various women.

DP: Did you act on your fantasies?

BOB: By God's grace I never actually committed fornication or adultery. When I got married, I was technically a virgin. I had been raised in a Christian home by loving parents who were active in Christian work. I had a good, nurturing background. At an early age I made a profession of faith. I really loved the Lord and sought to walk with God. As I began to struggle with sexuality from puberty onwards, I knew that looking at sexually explicit material and spinning fantasies were wrong. I was full of guilt and struggled a lot to overcome it.

God was gracious, and I overcame a lot of temptations. Sometimes I would go six months between indulgences in pornography. But the fantasy life and masturbation persisted for over twenty-five years. It is only in the past year that God has really helped me to come to terms with it and to experience the joy of consistently choosing purity. I've gained a deeper desire to overcome the sin of indulging in pornographic thought, and I've shut the door on the "tape library."

DP: Over the years, how often did you indulge in your fantasy images?

BOB: My thought life was an almost continuous struggle. Masturbation wasn't that frequent, but I was constantly on the prowl for images. I would look at women and tuck mental pictures away for future use. It was a type of hunting—hunting for a glimpse down a blouse or up a skirt. I was a sexual predator in my thought life, looking for prospects around me. I never acted it out to the point of adultery or even making advances towards someone. But my mind engaged in a secret life that I sought to have satisfy me, though I knew it couldn't and didn't satisfy. I would feel tremendously guilty and repent. On one level I was truly seeking to walk with God, seeking to avail myself of his grace. That's why I sought counseling ten years ago, even though I never really revealed the depths of the problem at that time. The pornography had such a tremendous hold on me that it constantly needed to be fueled through my eyes and imagination.

DP: How did your fantasy life affect your relationships with real people? Were all women equally victims or prey?

BOB: No, interestingly enough. There's a sense in which I sought the *Playboy* model type. Certain types of bodies didn't particularly appeal to me. But sometimes I could take someone who was not the type and seduce her in my mind anyway, even though she didn't have the characteristics that normally would attract me. I'd overlay the pornography on real people.

At the same time, there were many women whom I just liked as friends. If I saw someone as a friend, I saw her as a person rather than as a sex object. I didn't sexualize those relationships. Believe it or not, I could talk quite honestly about a lot of my struggles, even about lust in a general way, though not to the depth we're talking here. There were some men and women I just felt comfortable talking to; I really cared about them as people. Those friendships helped preserve and protect me from slipping deeper into the sin. I divided women into sex objects and friends, and the two categories never mixed together. The former were sexual objects to capture on mental videotape and fantasize about. The latter were just friends.

DP: How did your private world affect your relationships with your wife, children, and other family members?

BOB: I kept it secret. I don't think my children know about my struggles. Fortunately, God preserved me, so I didn't make my daughter in any way a sex object. I saw her as my daughter and respected her as that. As she grew up, I hated the thought of men doing to her what I did to other women, and I tried to protect her and inform her so she wouldn't be naive. It was the preservation of God that I never made her one of my objects of lust.

Without question, the influence of pornography sent powerful shock waves through my relationship to my wife. From early on I sinned by trying to improve her body, trying to get her to look more like Playmates. I realize that I was foolish and sinful; it was an attempt to feed those inner desires for the perfect body type. I think an even more serious sin was that often in making love to her, I'd use her as a launching pad for mental sexual adventures. Even today, having broken with indulgence in fantasy, I still occasionally have to fight off visual imagery. A little clip of a pornographic film will pop into my mind suddenly. Right in the moment I have to ask Jesus to help me get rid of it and love my wife for who she really is. So I do a lot of praying now.

DP: Did sexual immorality play out when you were in church?

BOB: Yes. Oftentimes I'd go to church and my eyes would sweep over the "singles row" or various women in the church who had become part of my fantasy. It was a way of, as it were, checking on my harem. I'd either invent new fantasies or just keep that fire hot in my soul by looking at them, gathering whatever I saw to use later on. Oftentimes the worship service was not a time for me to worship God, but my own lusts. Yet I'm thankful that usually I was at least battling against my sin. God helped me expose my sin to myself. I could see what was going on, and I would ask God to help me. He certainly did many times. But other times I did not ask him, and the church service became a time to fuel the fire inside, to feed the dragon of my soul.

DP: What has changed you over the past year, both in actual behavior and in fantasy? What's different and why?

BOB: Last year I'd been involved teaching a small group Bible study of men and women. We had talked in general about struggles and besetting sins. I had in a general way expressed my concerns about my own soul in the area of lust. Then in God's providence something re-markable happened. One of the younger married men in the group came to me and mentioned that he was on the verge of committing adultery. We got together later to talk at length. In a nutshell, he was willing to trash his marriage and his relationship with God for the sake of lust. I could identify, because on so many occasions I had seduced women in my mind. But this was not fantasy. This was real life. The person sitting across from me was actually about to commit adultery.

I was devastated because I identified with the sexual predator I saw in front of me. I realized we were well past the point where I could simply say to him, "Well, you know adultery is wrong and so forth. It's what the Bible says. . . ." I had to portray what it meant to be a sexual predator. This was not an academic explanation. I used a sort of shock therapy to show him what was going on in his mind. I got explicit. And finally I shocked him, and he suddenly recoiled from the prospect of committing adultery.

After that conversation he sought help from our pastor, and his marriage is on the mend. But I really think that *I* was the subject of that particular episode. God was dealing with me. God used me to help that man see what he was doing, but God was saying to me, "For years you thought of adultery and pornography as pleasurable, and you could enjoy it and entertain it in your heart. If you think it's so funny, then keep this man you've known for ten years from committing adultery and destroying his family." What was so devastating was that I had to reveal myself to save him. I had to hold myself out to public inspection. I think God was saying, "You can't serve two masters. You can't serve me and your sexual idolatry. You can't have both." Then in his electing love and good will, he made sure that I chose him.

DP: What helped you at that point when your choice came to a head? You've described the situation that God arranged, but what made it a decisive turning point? What truth mattered?

BOB: I think it was a deep awareness that God loved me, that Jesus had died for a sinful person. That was combined with the deep awareness that I was involved in a terrible sin. I was on an express train that was gaining speed on a collision course for a real tragedy. Jesus had loved me and would help me.

DP: What did you do in relationship to God?

BOB: I did a lot of praying and repenting. I asked for help and counsel and accountability. I needed protection from any temptation to indulge or incarnate the pornographic stuff I had in my mind, always available. I spent a lot of time praying that God would protect me. I made myself accountable to other people and made sure I was getting good advice. And Jesus helped me to make the choice to shut the door on voyeurism and fantasy.

This might sound like a little thing, but it was very significant to me, and it really captures how far God has brought me. Recently I was at an all-day conference for my job. As everyone was getting ready to leave, a woman in the row in front of me bent over to pick up her purse. The neckline of her blouse dropped open, revealing everything. Instead of looking, I turned away to pick up my own things . . . and praised Christ. I would have never turned away a year ago. You don't know how happy that makes me—to change!

DP: Some people would be dismayed that a professing Christian could be so double-minded with a lust problem for so many years. Were you a Christian?

BOB: I don't have any doubt that I was a Christian. I had availed myself of the means of grace for many years. I had meaningful times of worship. I hated my sins and repented. I had changed in many other areas, for example, financial integrity and dealing with anger. I had been growing in understanding what it meant to be a child of God and to let God control and command my life. I understood that God's providence is good, that I was not alone. I had learned in certain ways how to love my wife better. All these were truths that were having a growing influence in my life. I had even been spared worse sins, and had often successfully fought sexual temptation. But for various reasons, this particular kind of sexual obsession got a hold in me, and I let it stay there and grow.

DP: You fed the dragon.

Bob: Yes. When I experienced puberty and all those hormones were first running around in my body, I knew that I couldn't act on those desires because I was a Christian. I knew it was wrong. So instead, I tried to contain it in my own soul. It was like building a container vessel for a secret and seductive pleasure. I didn't act on it overtly, but I stuffed the struggle inside and created a dragon. It kept demanding more and more of my time and energy. But I still think God's hand was on me to protect me from ever actually committing adultery or pursuing other forms of pornography, such as child porn. He let me struggle to show me that I had to put him first. I was willing to put God first in lots of areas, but not in this. The problem was I *liked* pornography. I still like it, in the sense that the temptations are there and I could be seduced by it. I know that vigilance on my part and walking with God in his love and protective power will enable me to defeat my evil. I feel my vulnerability, but I know Jesus has helped me change.

DP: One extreme believes that being a Christian should eliminate a struggle like this, immediately or totally. The other extreme believes that being a Christian really doesn't make any difference. *Is* there a difference because you are a Christian? If so, what is the difference? To the world, sexual lust is a given, so why fight? Why be uptight about it? How do you know you're really different?

BOB: Let me use the metaphor of my eroticized soul becoming a toxic waste dump. I had tried to contain the obsession with pornography in the waste dump. But the toxic waste was leaking out. It was corrosive, and it seeped through the walls. In my relationships I sometimes wondered whether I was operating in a seductive, predatory mode or a wholesome, relational mode.

Would I commit adultery if I had an opportunity? Would I go on to molest children? Would I get aroused homosexually? I saw I was capable of anything. But now, though that tension is still there between predation and love, it has lessened considerably. Often it seems gone. I want different things in relationship to people. I can honestly say that loving concern, and not hunting for opportunities to indulge, much more characterizes me.

Since last year, God has enabled me not to indulge in mental sexual adventure, or lewd jokes, or pornography. That shock therapy I experienced in seeing what I really was and where it led, and seeing how much Christ loved me, has simply shut the whole thing down. It doesn't mean I don't have the impulse sometimes. But now the capacity to say, "No, I want you, Lord, and not that. You are most important, and I can't have you halfheartedly," has been really enhanced. It's nothing that came out of me. God's love broke the shackles, the bondage to this sexual idol, and caused me to cry out to him for help. He keeps reminding me that I must keep relying on him.

DP: You've described saying no to sin and yes to God. Have there been other behavioral changes of the positive sort?

BOB: As I've said, the putting off of sin includes not masturbating anymore and not indulging in sexual fantasy. And I have consciously treasured my relationship with Jesus. Also on the positive side, God has been dealing with much more than lust. I've been learning to love my wife. That's much wider than just sex.

DP: What does that change look like?

BOB: It means asking God to help me to put her first, not my own agenda. It means trusting my welfare to God when my wife doesn't do what I want. It means I don't have to demand that she change, or get angry at her, or manipulate her, in lots of ways besides the sexual. I'm seeing a lot more of my sins besides sexual obsession, and Christ is helping me slowly to change. I know I've become less angry. I don't withdraw into self-pity and lick my wounds. Before, when my wife let me down, I would retreat into self-pity, and then the door to my private video room would beckon with private pleasure. Not falling into self-pity has been one more nail that keeps that door shut tight.

I think I've become more honest and constructive, instead of either avoiding my wife or attacking her. I used to get self-righteous, and even use Bible verses to criticize her. I've got a long way to go, but I can see that the opposite of that selfish world of lust is not just sexual purity; it's learning what it really means to love someone. I asked God to help me see my wife as a person, not as a sex object. He has helped me do that. He has helped me to love her sex-

ually and put her first. I've also learned to forgive her for things she has done to me. I had
built up a lot of fear and resentment. To see
that God has forgiven me has helped a tremendous amount. I've committed some terrible
sins. Therefore, I really want to freely forgive
her. When we have disagreements, I don't feel
so compelled to defend myself because I have a
fresh awareness of God's love for me and his
working out a victory in my life in overcoming
sin. I feel so forgiven. All these have really
helped, and they enable me not to judge her.

DP: Why didn't counseling bring a break-
through ten years ago? What went wrong that
made it only partially helpful?

BOB: When I went to the counselor, I told
him there were problems. But in some ways I
spoke in code; I was not explicit enough as to
what my sexual problems were. I said I struggled with lust, but everybody struggles with
lust. It would have been helpful if the counselor had been more specific in his questions.
Exactly what's going on here? Are you masturbating? Are you engaged in pornography? To
what extent? What kind? How do you treat
women? What are your fantasies?

The counseling did give me hope and
helped me get a more constructive perspective
on my marriage at the time. But what was lack-

ing was that I never really came to see that I was trying to serve two masters. The significance of my struggle with lust never came home to me until a year ago. For me, the basic idolatrous self-worship expressed itself in pornographic fantasy. In somebody else it might be a career, or making money, or getting married, or whatever else, always putting yourself first and trying to control the world and playing God. Perhaps if discussions had broadened out ten years ago to see that I really desired to be first, that I was putting myself first and sought power and pleasure, it would have helped. My desire for self-worship was really finding its expression in sexual fantasy.

Over the intervening years my pastor has preached that the primary issue in adultery is that you want someone else to worship you and serve you, to be at your beck and call. That resonated with me. I could see that theme in my fantasies. My pastor's preaching was really used of God to help me to see more clearly and to define the real battles. For years God has been setting me up for the cataclysmic experience of seeing myself for what I really was, that I might learn to die to myself through Jesus' grace.

Something else the counselor might have done is probably less important but also might have helped. I told him I thought that there were some things in my past that might have contributed to this struggle, but we didn't pursue it very far. It was all pretty fuzzy to me at the time. Since then I've come to understand some things in my background better. An incident when I was molested by a baby sitter, several voyeuristic incidents where I witnessed naked women, and the reading of *Playboy* were all incidents that I think contributed to patterning my sexual sins towards an obsession with breasts, with oral sex, and with blondes. Recognizing how my pattern of sexual obsessions first developed its particular shape helped the tumblers fall into place for me in terms of understanding myself. With that incident of molestation, I was abused, but I'm grateful that I never got stuck in feeling like a victim or thinking that it caused me to sin. That incident didn't make me sin, but it might have affected what objects my lust gravitated towards. Looking at those particular events has helped me understand how some of my particular preferences and attractions might have been formed. It helps me to be aware of where I am tempted.

DP: What passages or themes of Scripture have helped most in your struggle and the changes you have experienced?

BOB: So many pieces of truth have played a part: Christ's love, understanding sexual sin as sin, understanding my idolatry of sexual power and pleasure, God's providence. James 4:6 has really come to life: "God resists the proud but gives grace to the humble." That tells me to ask for help without some big explanation for why I need help. When I'm in the thick of the fight, whatever it is I'm struggling with, I can humbly cry out to God, "Help! I'm in trouble. Right now I'm being seduced by the dragon of my soul. Help." If I try to fight in my own strength, it usually leads to catastrophe. In the battle for my mind to walk with God, to be holy and pure, I need to commune with Christ all the time. It's not just a matter of devotional times. It's when the battle rages. I've often incorporated that Scripture into my conversation with God. Many times when I've fallen, I didn't do that. I wasn't honest with God about my need.

DP: That expresses perfectly what James says a couple of sentences earlier, "You don't have because you don't ask." In a way, it's what the entire book is about: "If any man lacks wisdom, let him ask God, who gives generously and without reproach."

BOB: Right. I need to ask God to help me pay attention to the little things that can snowball into the full force of temptation. For example, if I'm working where a lot of young women are present, I need to bring God into it. "Where is my mind? Am I going to savor their profiles? Will I view these women as persons or sex objects? Help me to see them as needing your love." I need to see them as women who need to know Jesus, just like me, not as shapes that my eyes can devour.

The other thing that has really meant a lot has been being honest and accountable to people. It was very humbling—humiliating—to admit how ugly my inner world really became. But the encouragement of my faith, the knowledge that someone would ask me a searching question and I couldn't lie meant a lot. I was always inclined to be a Lone Ranger Christian. Through the preaching of my church, I began to share the struggle with a couple of people. That was very helpful. Having to rely in part on other people kept reminding me that I was not fighting this battle in my own strength but relying upon Christ.

DP: Hebrews 3:13 says, "Encourage one another daily" so that we don't fall away from God and into sin. You are describing very basic things about the Christian life that we often don't put into practice.

BOB: That's right. Let me say one more thing about temptations. The small things are precursors to the big things. If I bring lust in past the first gate, the gate of the eye, it becomes a far greater battle for me. God has been building strong fortifications behind the first eye gate, but he keeps saying to me, "Don't let it go through the first gate." God has purged out lots of junk in the last year and taken up residence in some great new ways. He has helped me to put on Christ and love people, seeking ways that don't put my own agenda, my own poison, first.

I used to live saying to God, "You can have some of my life, but I really want this little indulgence. I like this too much. It gives me a sense of power. It's a perfect world that I can create. Things always go exactly my way. People do exactly what I want. I'm always on top." Fantasy is a great ego-feeder.

I remember a sermon where my pastor asked the question, "Can you say to God, 'Do whatever it takes to save me' in the full sense of that word?" I remember sitting there and saying to God, "Do whatever it takes. I'm sick of a double life." I remember being afraid when I said that, thinking that God would do something like take one of my children or send me a catastrophic disease or something of that nature. That's what I thought "whatever it takes" would mean.

God was much more clever! He took me personally into the fire of my sin and put the screws to me, putting me in a situation that he had chosen in love, and he made sure I made the right choice to tear the mask off my sin. By making the choice to defend God's honor that night, I had to own up publicly to a brother in Christ that sexual sin was very, very wrong.

DP: That reminds me of another part of James. God placed a mirror in front of your face and forced you to see yourself. Then, when you articulated how ugly lust really is, for the sake of loving another person, that conviction of sin began an avalanche of changes.

BOB: Right. I portrayed myself in the light both to him and to myself. Sexual obsession had been my particular form of trying to be God in my own life. A friend of mine once said, "Indulging in pornography is like getting a fix of cocaine or some other drug. You feel the high. When you come down, you feel so awful and you say, 'I'll never do that again.' But then you want the fix." I went through that cycle a thousand times: the excitement of sin, the misery, and then the craving would come back. It was intoxicatingly powerful because it was more than just sex. It was worship, self-worship. But Jesus Christ is more powerful. Once I got honest, I found grace.